THIS BRIDESMAID NEEDS A MOTHER FUCKING DRINK

ASIDE FROM THE WEDDING

BEING A BRIDESMAID IS FUCKING AWESOME

NOT JUST A BRIDESMAID

A MOTHERFUCKING LEGEND

BRIDESMAIDS

GET SHIT DONE

THIS BRIDESMAID

IS HAPPY A.F.

BRIDESMAIDS ARE THE DOG'S BOLLOCKS

BRIDESMAID*

*BECAUSE KICKASS MIRACLE WORKER IS NOT AN OFFICIAL JOB TITLE.

YOU MUST BE MISTAKING ME FOR A BRIDESMAID WHO GIVES A S[HIT]

THIS BRIDESMAID NEEDS A MOTHERFUCKING NAP

YOU MUST BE MISTAKING ME FOR A BRIDESMAID WHO

GIVES A SHIT

THIS BRIDESMAID NEEDS A MOTHERFUCKING NAP

YODA BEST DAMN BRIDESMAID

I'M A SUPER bridesmaid

What's Your Fucking Superpower?

THIS BRIDESMAID IS A MOTHERFUCKING DELIGHT

THIS BRIDESMAID IS FRESH OUT OF FUCKS

THIS BRIDESMAID COULD GIVE A RAT'S ASS

BRIDESMAIDS CARE A WHOLE FUCKING LOT

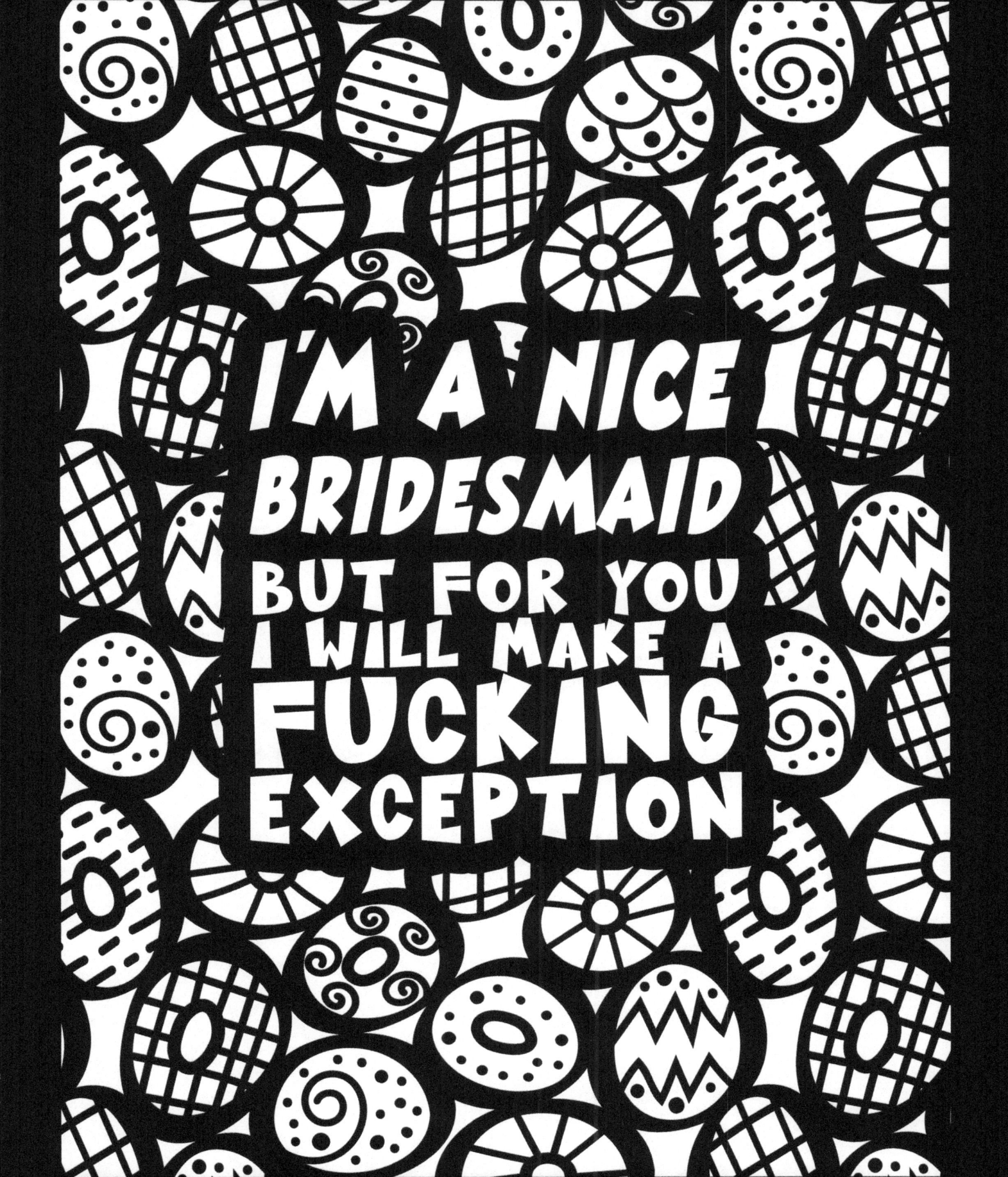

I'M A NICE BRIDESMAID BUT FOR YOU I WILL MAKE A FUCKING EXCEPTION

BRIDESMAIDS ARE FUCKING AWESOME

THIS BRIDESMAID IS DONE HELPING ASSHOLES TODAY

WHO THE FUCK SAID BEING A BRIDESMAID WOULD BE EASY?

YEAH, BASICALLY I LISTEN TO PEOPLE COMPLAIN.

SIP SIP HOORAY

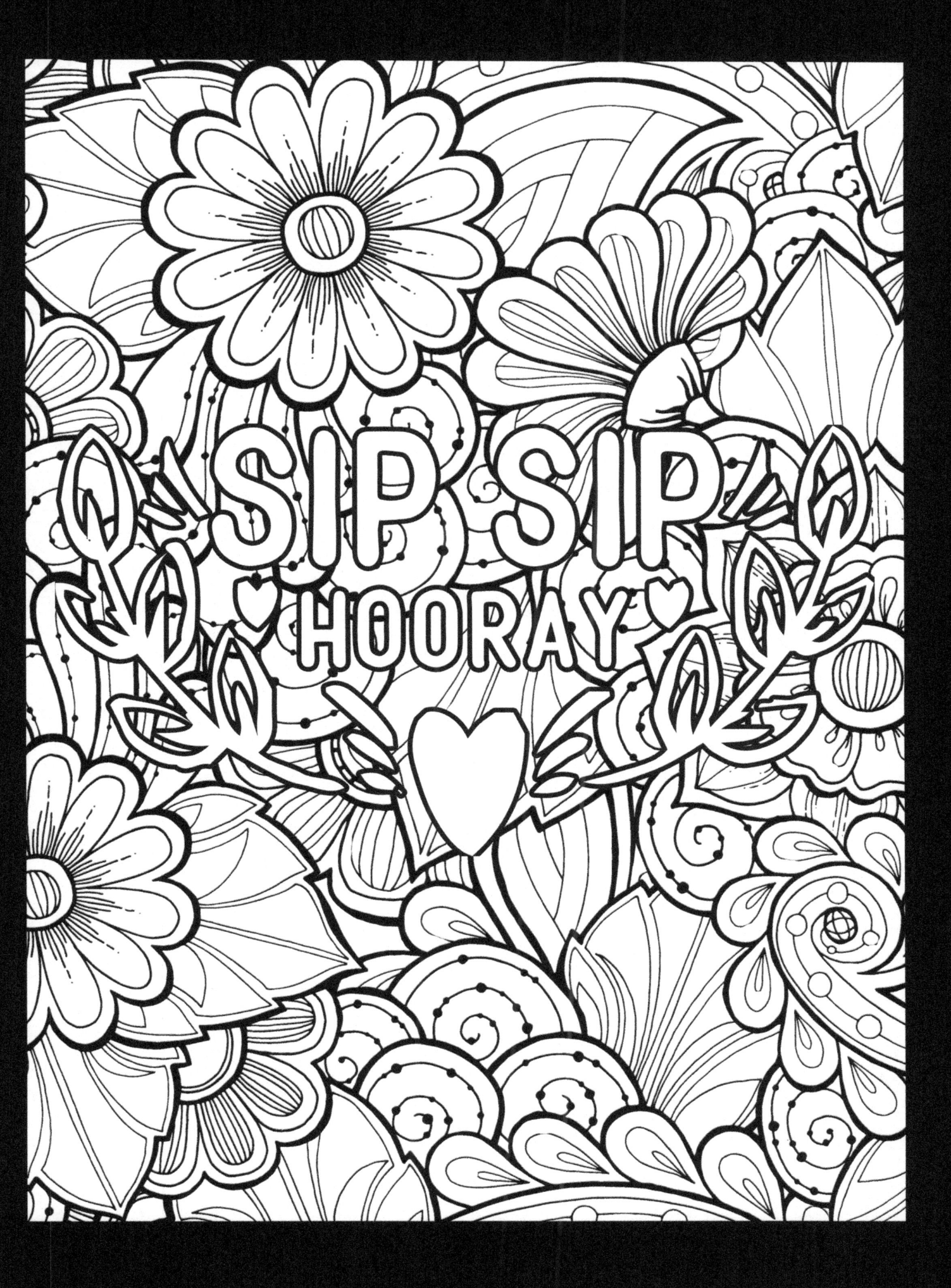

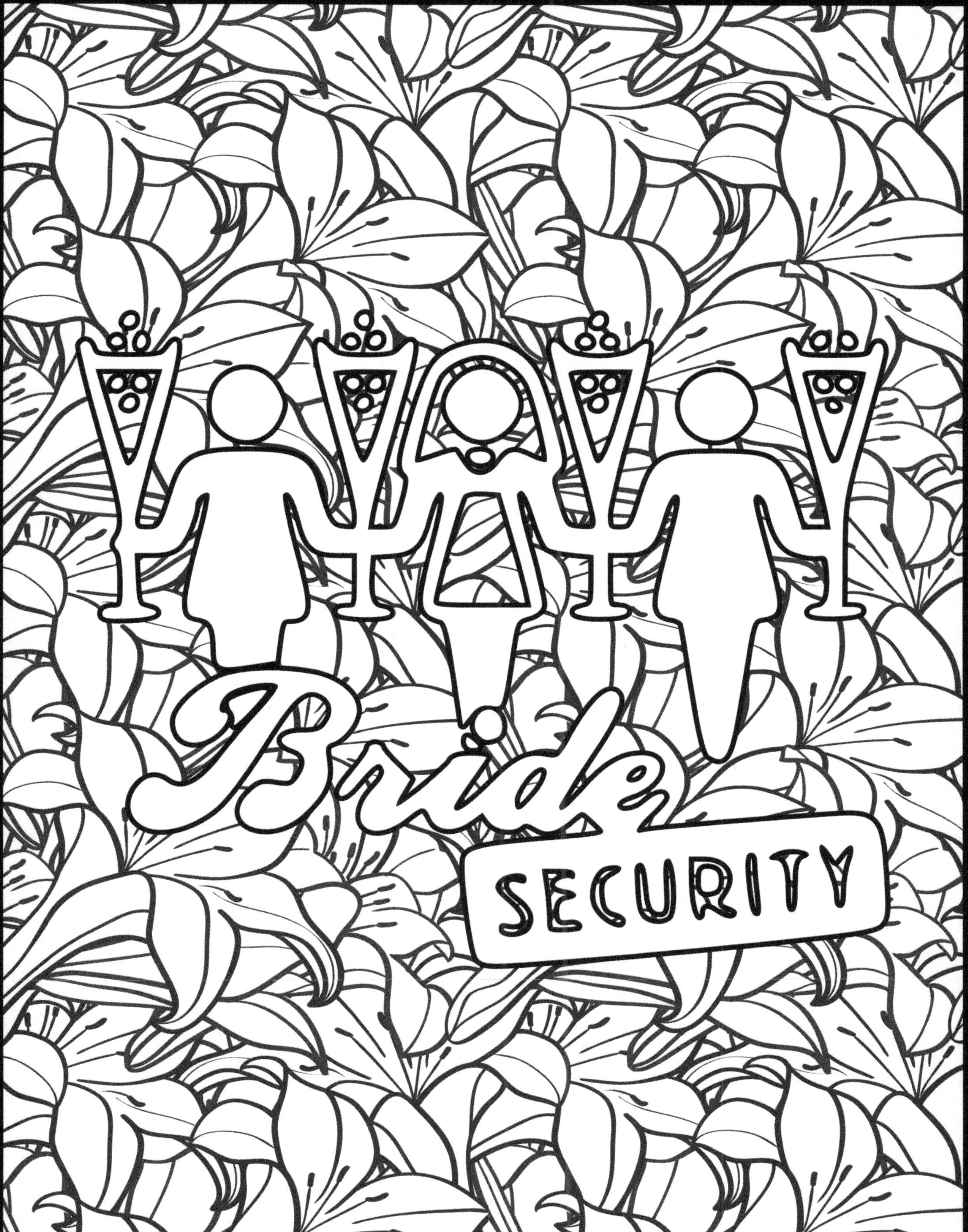

Bride
SECURITY

Bride's Crew

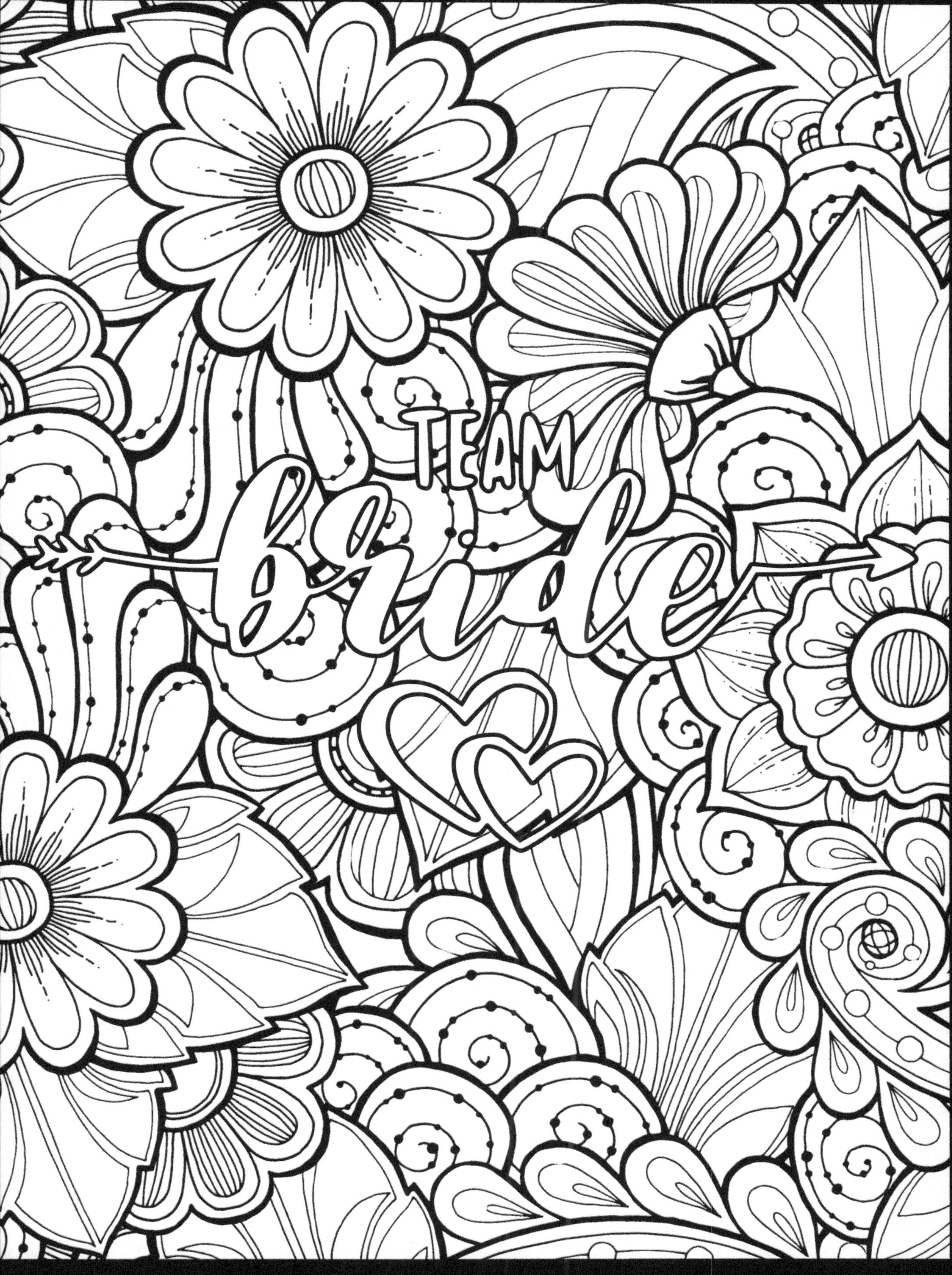
TEAM
bride

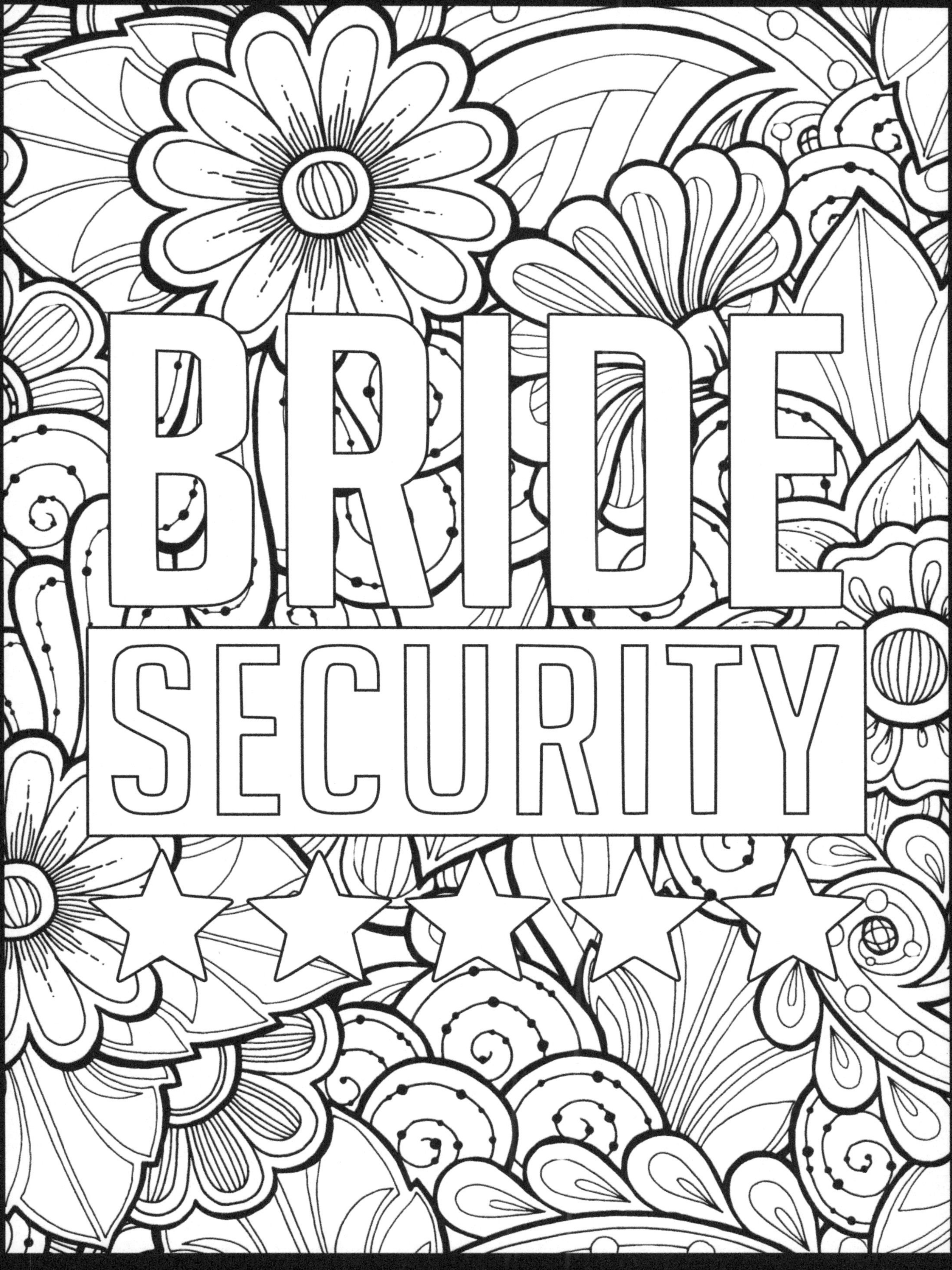
BRIDE
SECURITY

BRIDE SUPPORT TEAM

BRIDE groom

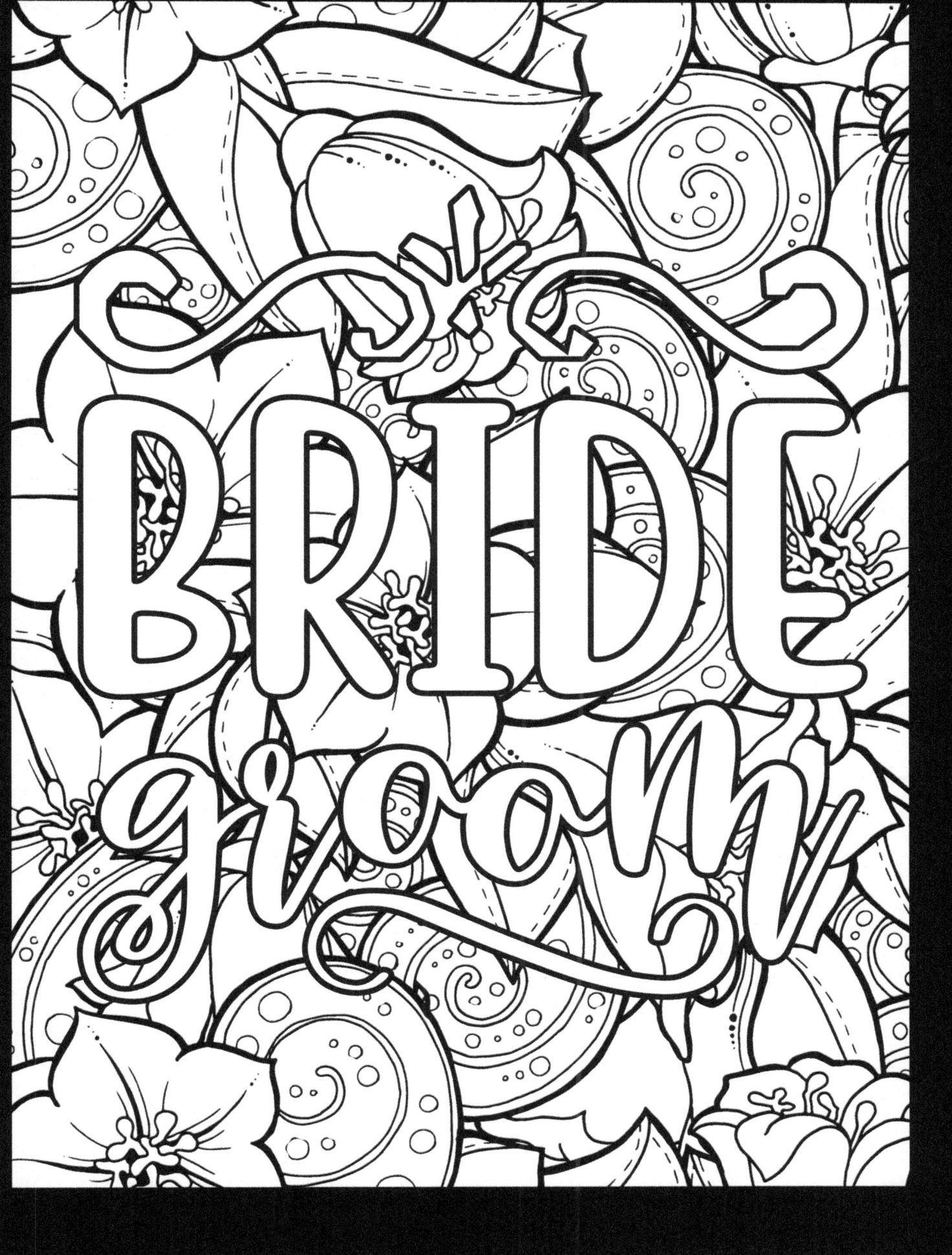

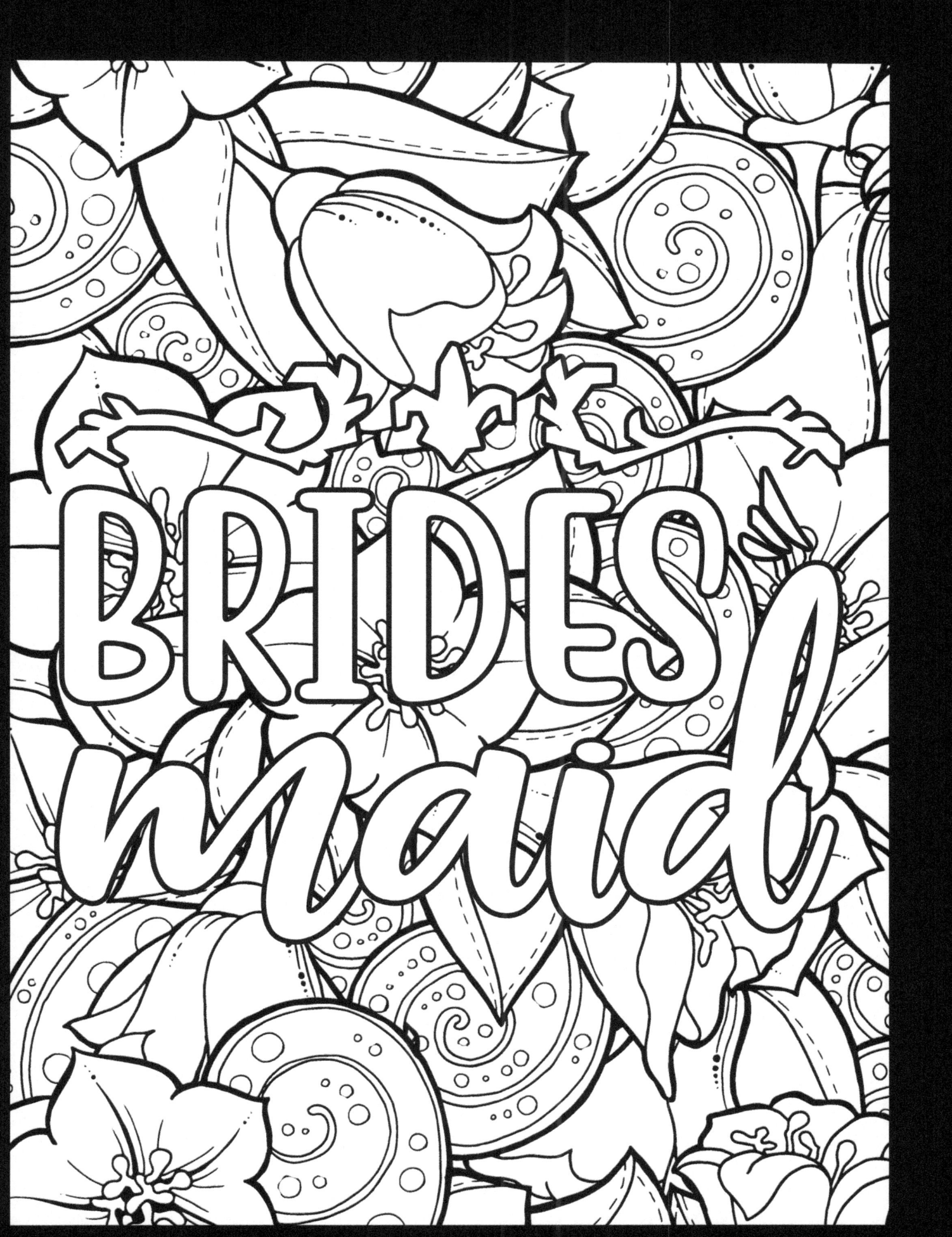

BRIDES*maid*

BRIDE SECURITY

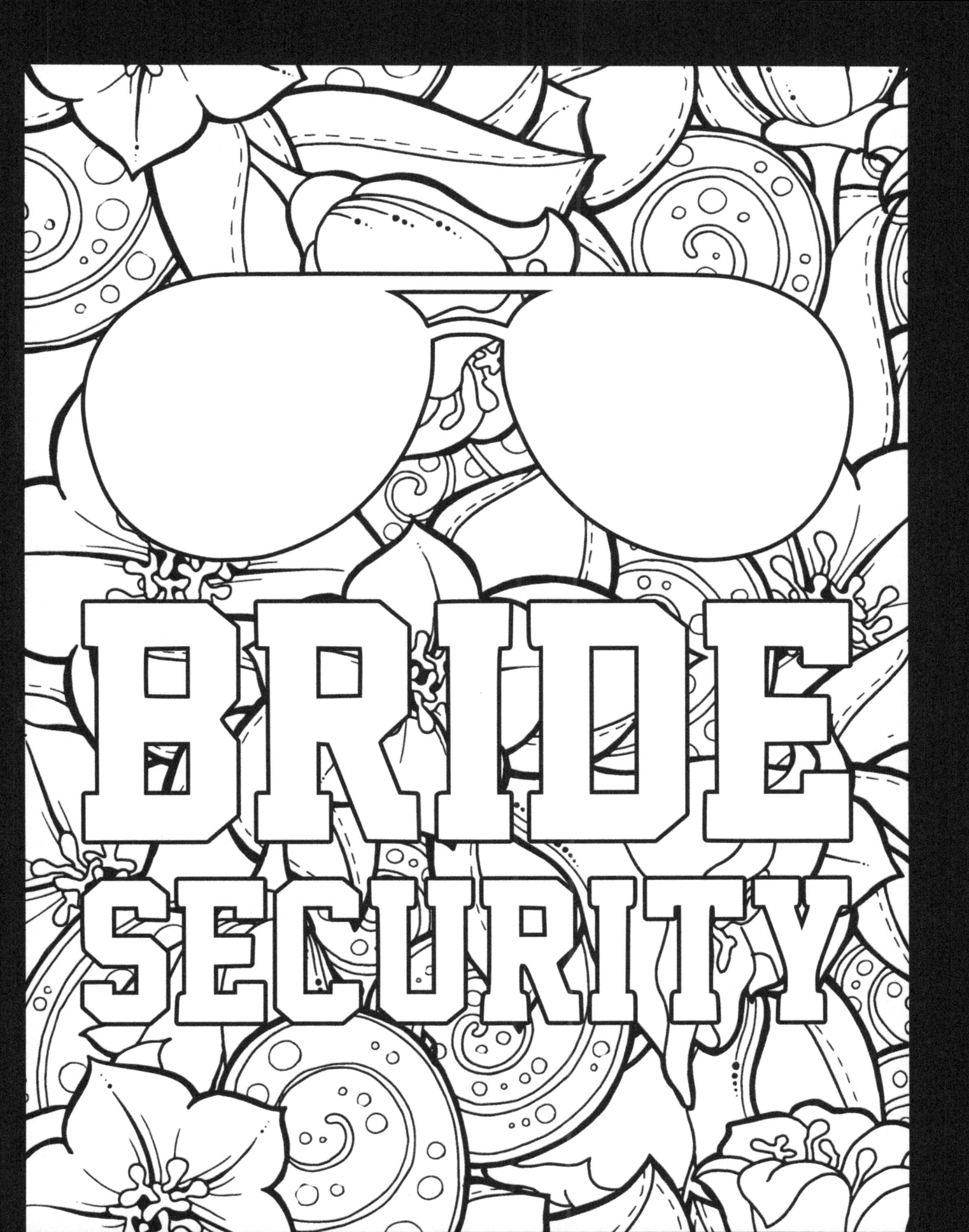

Bride Squad

LAST fling BEFORE the ring

BRIDE SQUAD

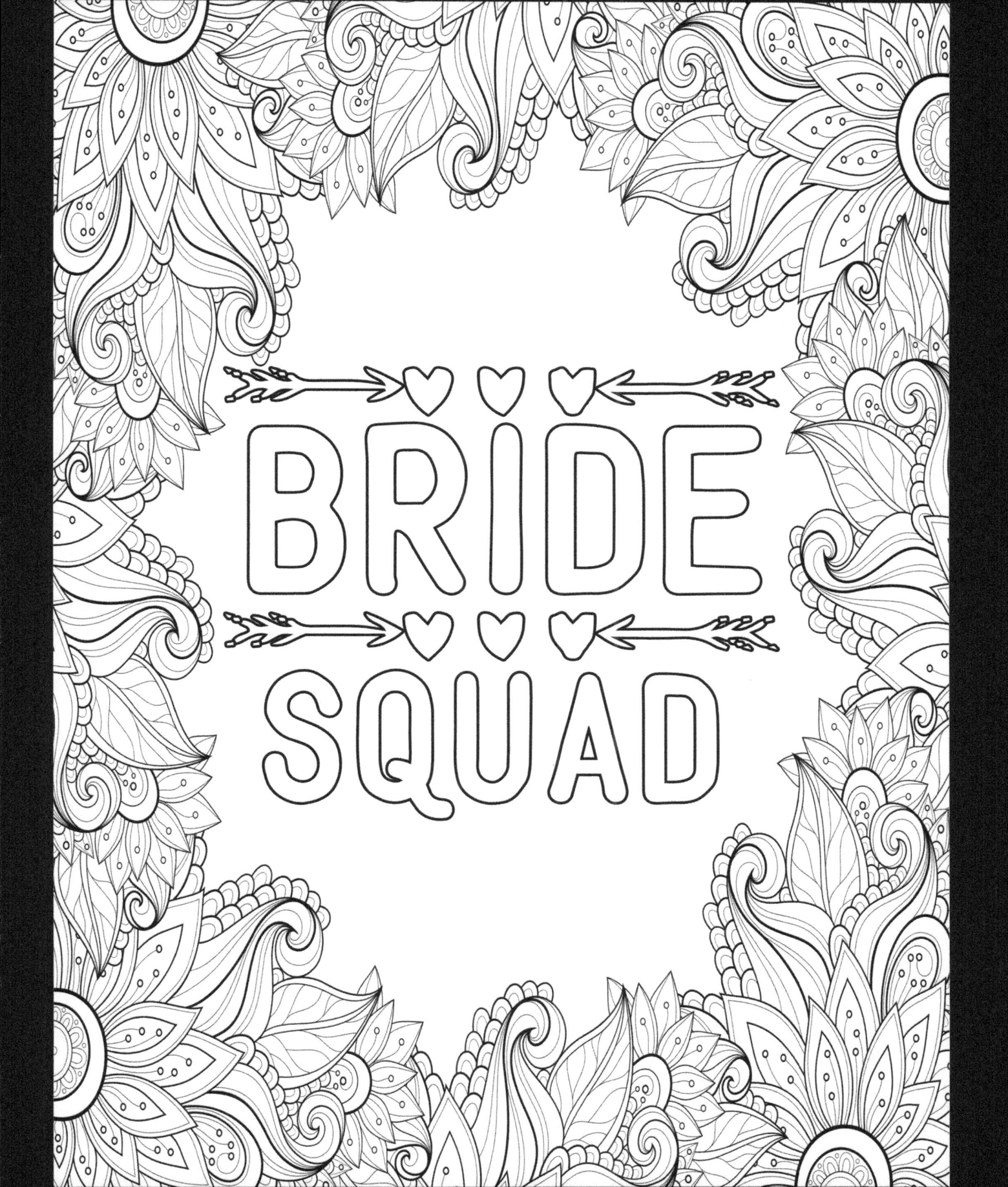

My Chosen Wanted and Cherished

sip sip hooray

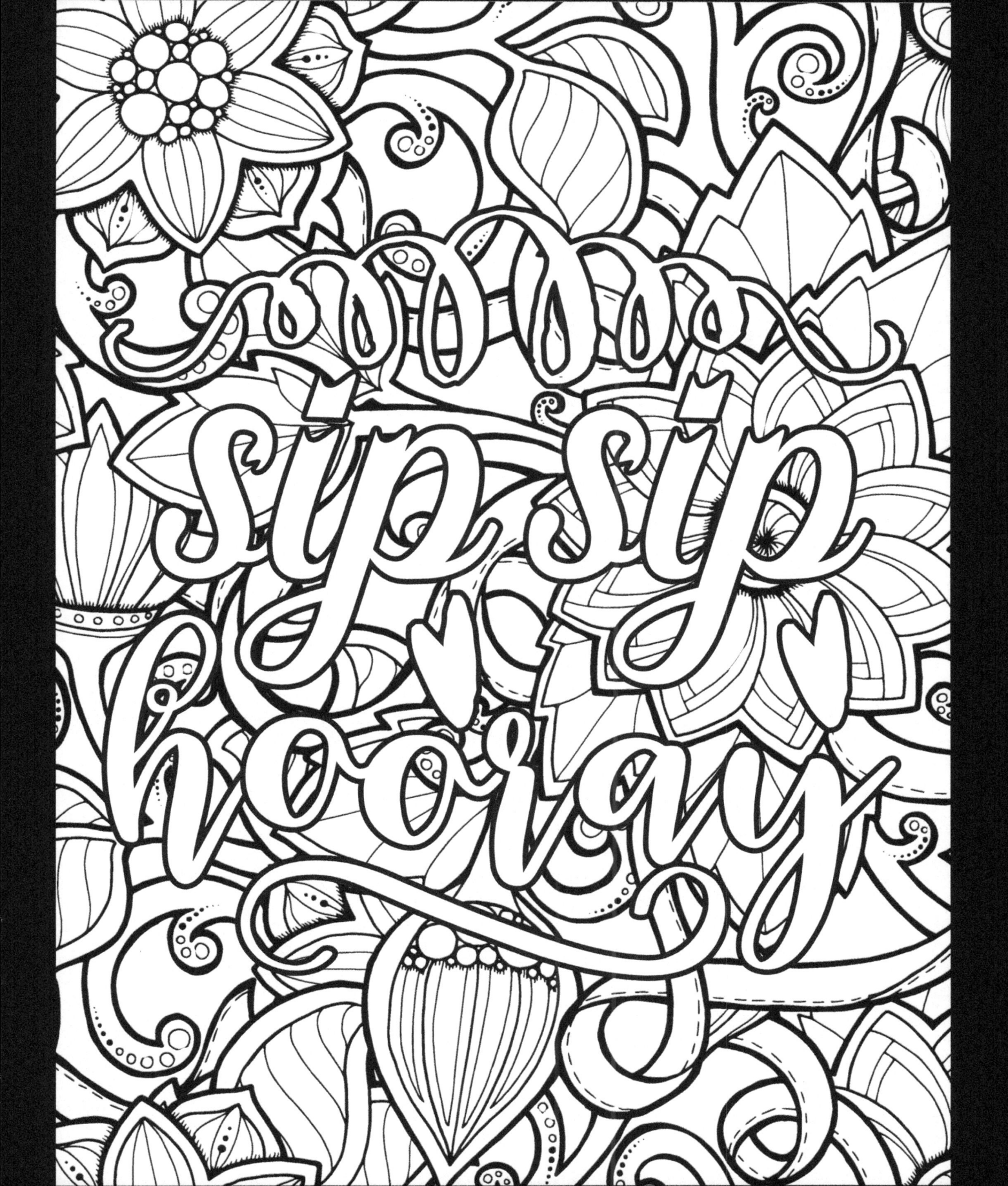

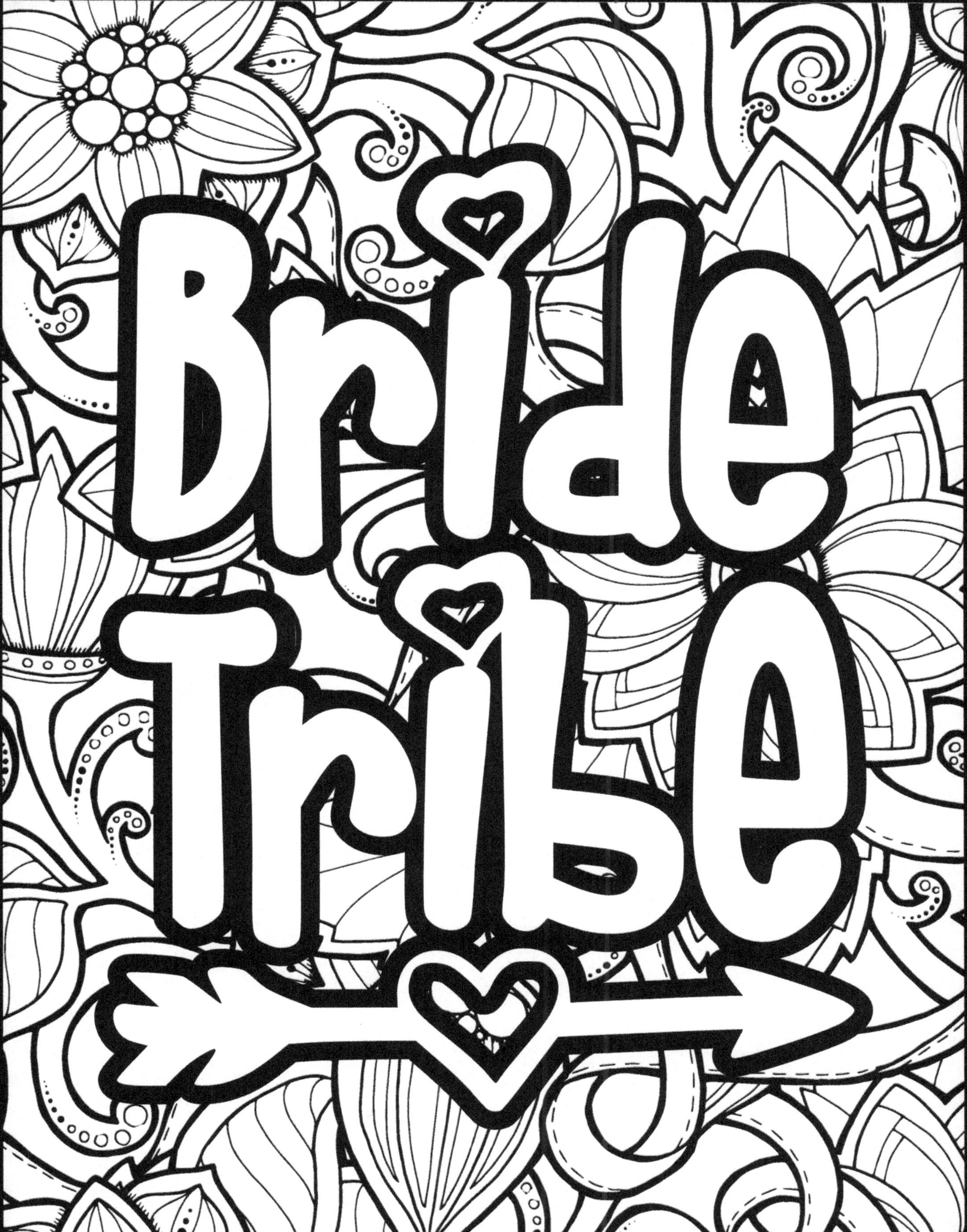
Bride
Tribe

HEN PARTY

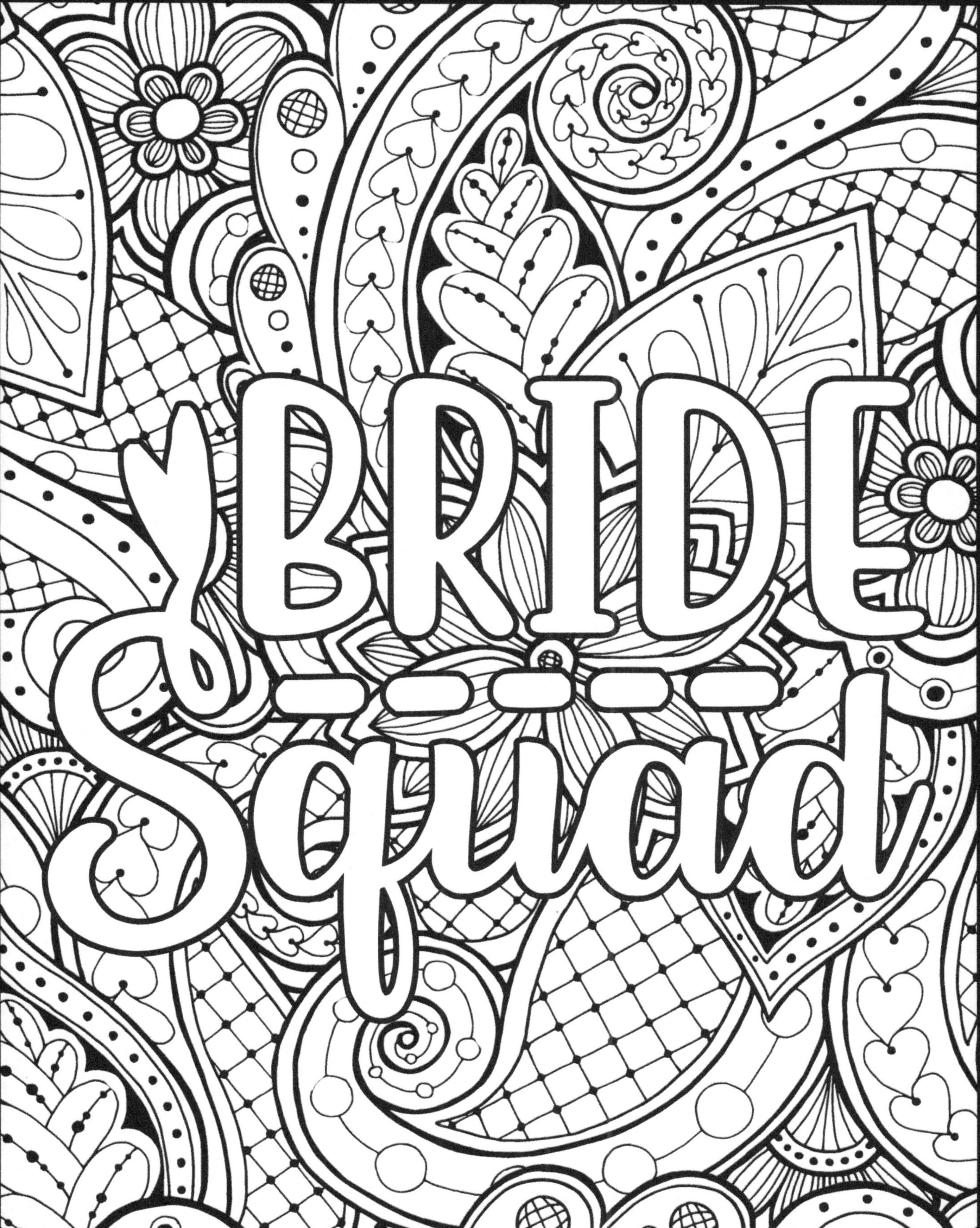
BRIDE
Squad

BRIDE TRIBE

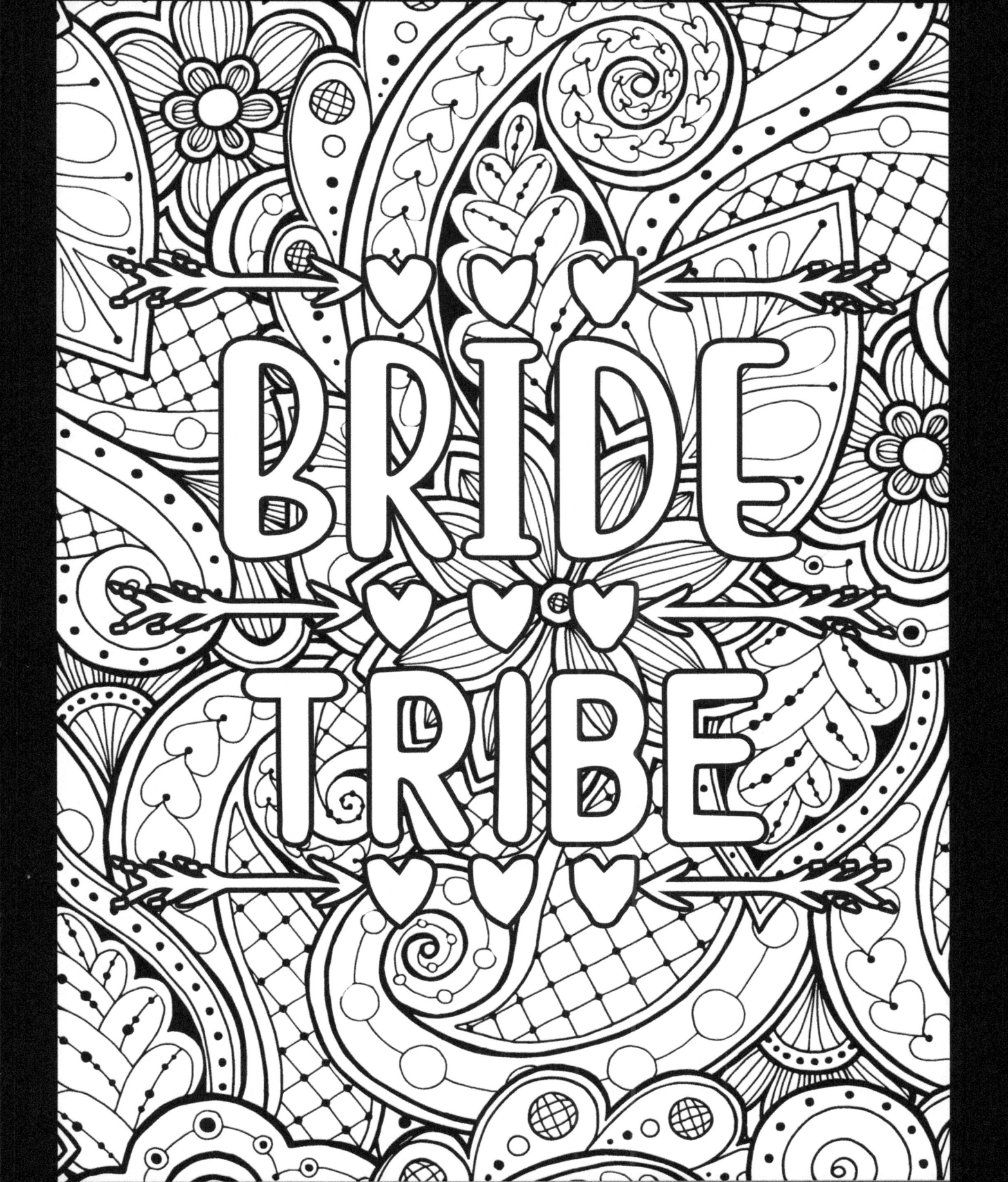

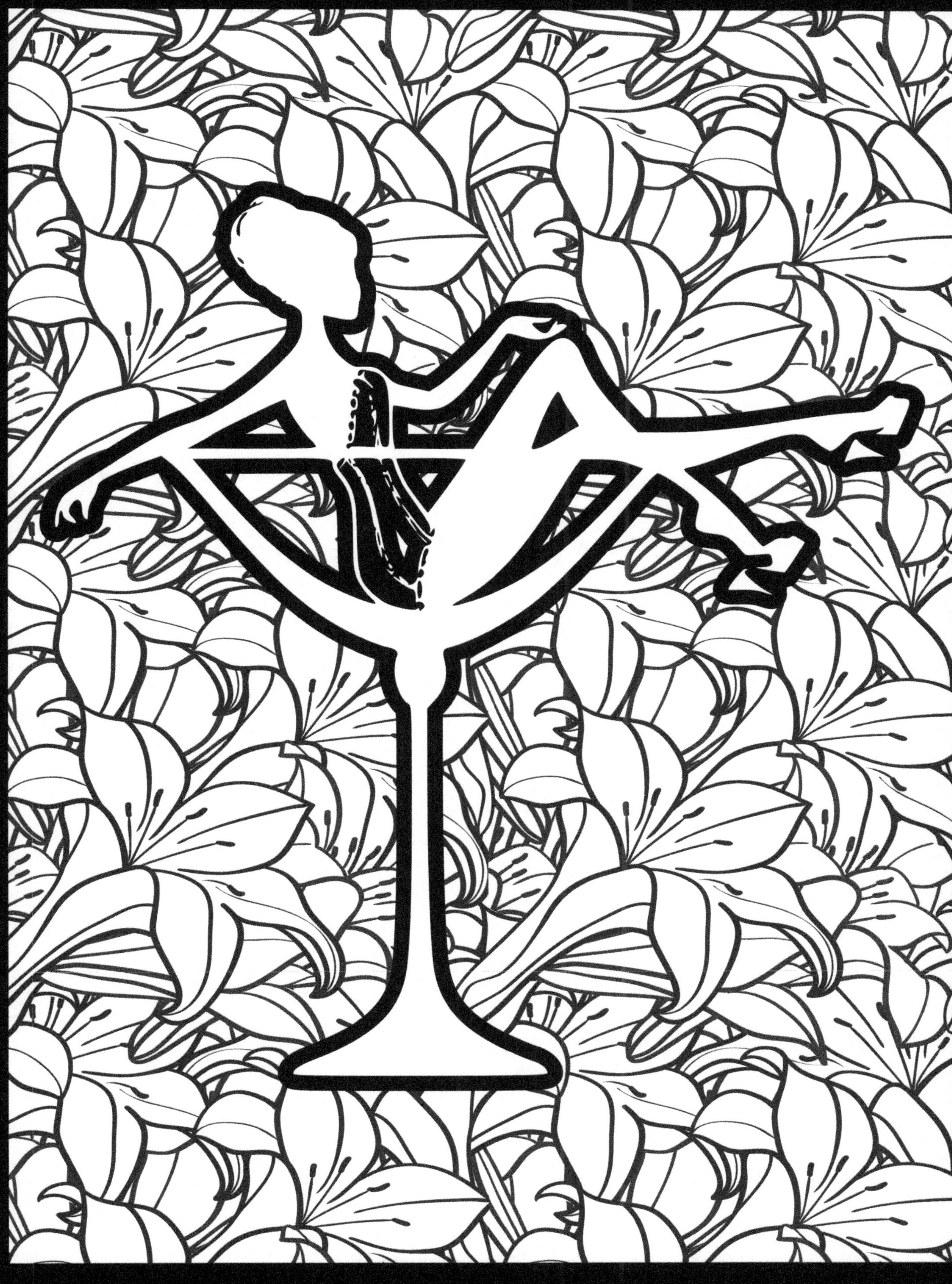

Hen Party

Oh Dear

I forgot to give a fuck.

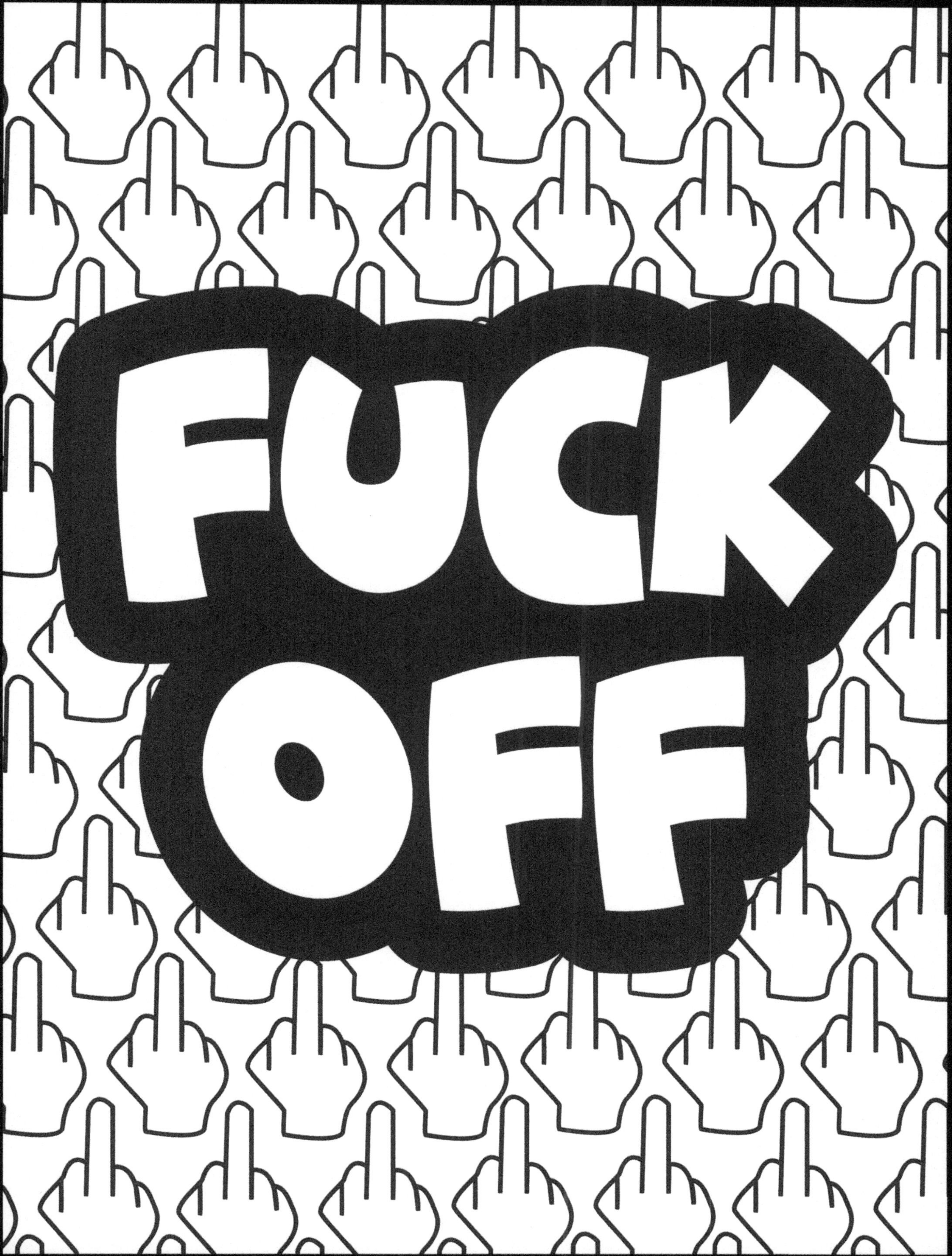
FUCK
OFF

THE PATH OF INNER PEACE BEGINS WITH FOUR WORDS

NOT MY FUCKING PROBLEM

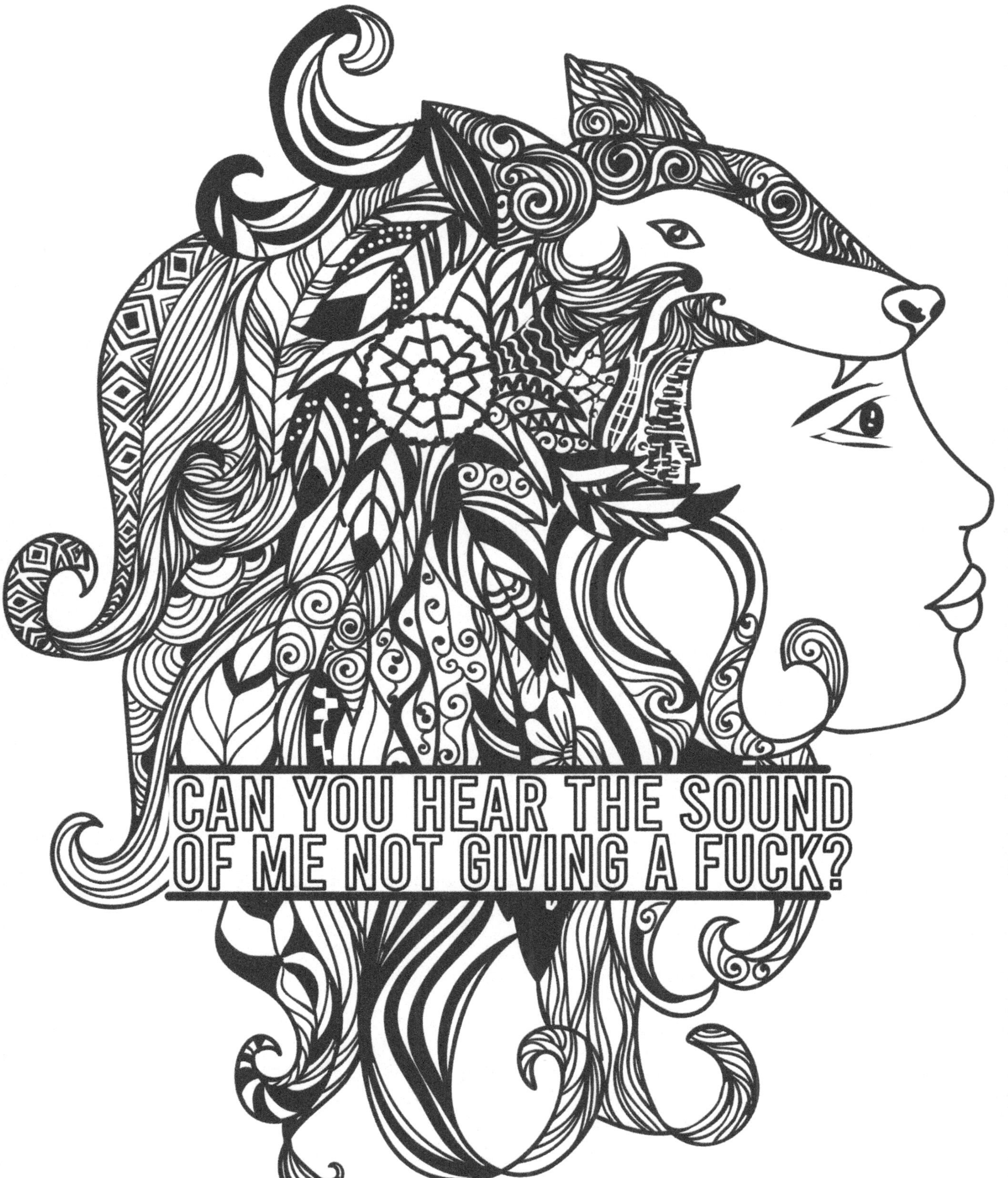
CAN YOU HEAR THE SOUND
OF ME NOT GIVING A FUCK?

LET'S GET THE FUCK OUT OF HERE

UTTER BULLSHIT

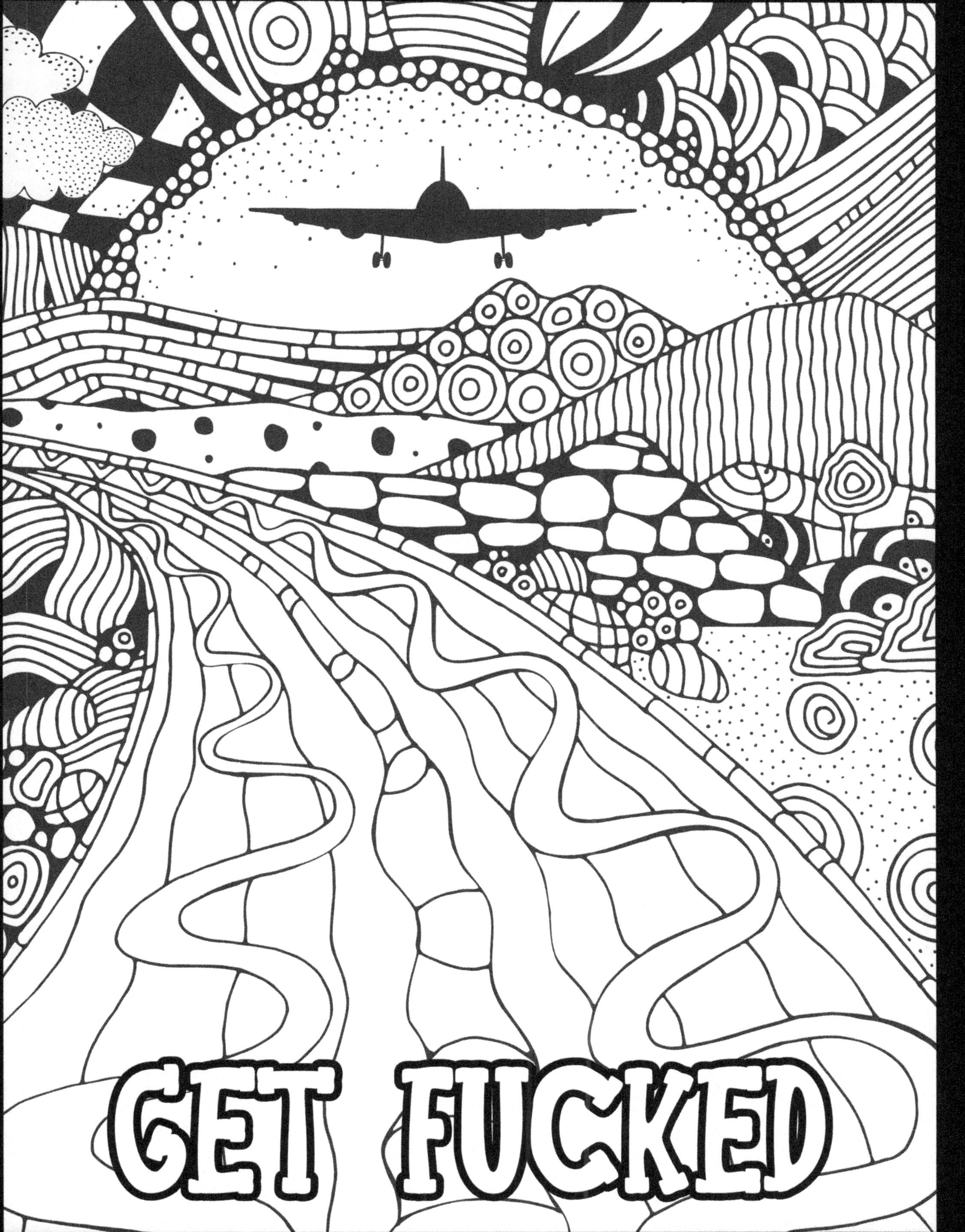
GET FUCKED

SEE IF I FUCKING CARE

LEAVE ME THE FUCK ALONE

FUCKITY FUCK FUCK FUCK

Made in the USA
Las Vegas, NV
22 December 2021